insight

University of Illinois

Photographs by Don Hamerman

DH BOOKS

Contents

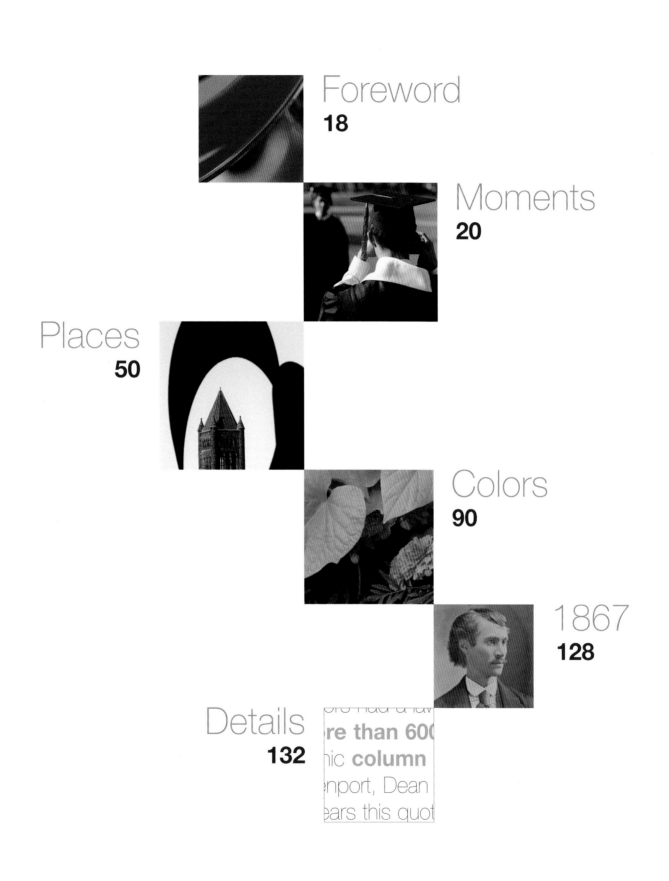

...rs had a lav...
re than 600
...hic **column**
...nport, Dean
...ears this quot...

Champaign County is so flat they actually built a hill in Crystal Lake Park. The soybean fields reach out in all directions, green carpets with farmhouses and trees dotted on the horizon. The campus of the University of Illinois at Urbana-Champaign is flat, too, which explains why it has more wheelchair students than almost anywhere else. Boulder has mountains, Madison has the lake, Cornell is far above Cayuga's waters, but what Urbana-Champaign (my home town) has is sun and shade, the seasons, the reassurance of Georgian architecture that rests with confidence on the prairie, and a certain no-nonsense seriousness that has made this not only one of the largest universities in the world but one of the best.

The key words in the previous sentence are "home town." I grew up on Washington Street. I went to St. Mary's Grade School and Urbana High School. As a high school senior, I was in an early admission program, and plunged into the basement of Altgeld Hall three days a week to take a freshman Verbal Communications class. I vibrated with excitement. There was for me an energy about the campus that has never left. Four days before writing these words, I walked slowly across the Quadrangle in the early morning and breathed carefully, as if inhaling the past.

My father was an electrician who worked for the University. When the lights went out on campus during an electrical storm, he would roust me in the middle of the night and we would drive through rain or hailstones to the power plant, where he would tell me to stand by the door and watch as he turned the lights back on. When they repaired the bells in Altgeld's tower 10 years ago, they found a note signed by Walter Ebert and three other electricians who had done the job the last time. My dad never taught me a thing about being an electrician. He came home and lectured me at dinner: "I was in the English Building today, and saw the professors with their feet up on their desks, reading books and smoking their pipes. Boy, that's the job for you!" That sounded good to me. I was an English and Journalism major, read a lot of books, put my feet on a lot of desks, never started with the pipe. Working for *The Daily Illini*, I put out the paper one night a week, a 3 a.m. deadline, and would drive home or walk to the Phi Delt house through the silent streets. When it snowed there was a hush.

These wonderful, evocative photographs by Don Hamerman bring back my memories, and those of anyone who attended the University in Urbana-Champaign. Illinois is not only a great university but a great school—a Big Ten school, with a stadium that seats 70,000 in a town that, when I was growing up, didn't have that many people. It is like a magnet for the best high school students, and on

a weekend if you walk through the Illini Union you will meet kids in town for the state speech contest, or the math finals, or for music or science, filmmaking or computers, acting or agriculture. In my time the Quadrangle was deeply shaded by towering elms, and then they were struck down by disease, and new trees were planted, and now there is shade again. I went to summer school two different summers, and loved the way classes were small and drowsy, and sometimes held on the grass, and there were concerts from the Auditorium steps. In the winter, I went to the film societies, and found out about movies before I knew they would be my job.

I look at Hamerman's photos and remember things that happened here, and there. I see the staircases and corridors and remember going to classes, and visiting professors. My future was in those buildings, and I knew it. Some of his photos are of sculptures by Lorado Taft. He was an Urbana boy, too. So was Mark Van Doren. Rabindranath Tagore, the great Bengali poet, attended Illinois. Since the earliest years, students from all over the world have studied there, and Hamerman's photos, if they could talk, would speak in many accents. In the early days the campus was in the middle of nowhere – not near the courthouse in Urbana or the Illinois Central station in Champaign, but in a great muddy field linked by a horse-drawn omnibus. The original bus shelter now stands just south of the Natural History Building, and is one of the oldest structures on campus. Harker Hall, a few steps away, is the oldest major building.

Anyone returning to Urbana-Champaign after 20 years would be startled by the changes. There is another Quadrangle now where Illini Field once stood. Enormous buildings have grown up north and south of the original campus. But the old landmarks still stand, the bells of Altgeld still ring, you can still bike or picnic on the South Farms, students still nap on the couches in the Union, and they sing songs late at night on the Quad. And you would be amazed how many people, all over the world, are loyal to you, Illinois.

Moments

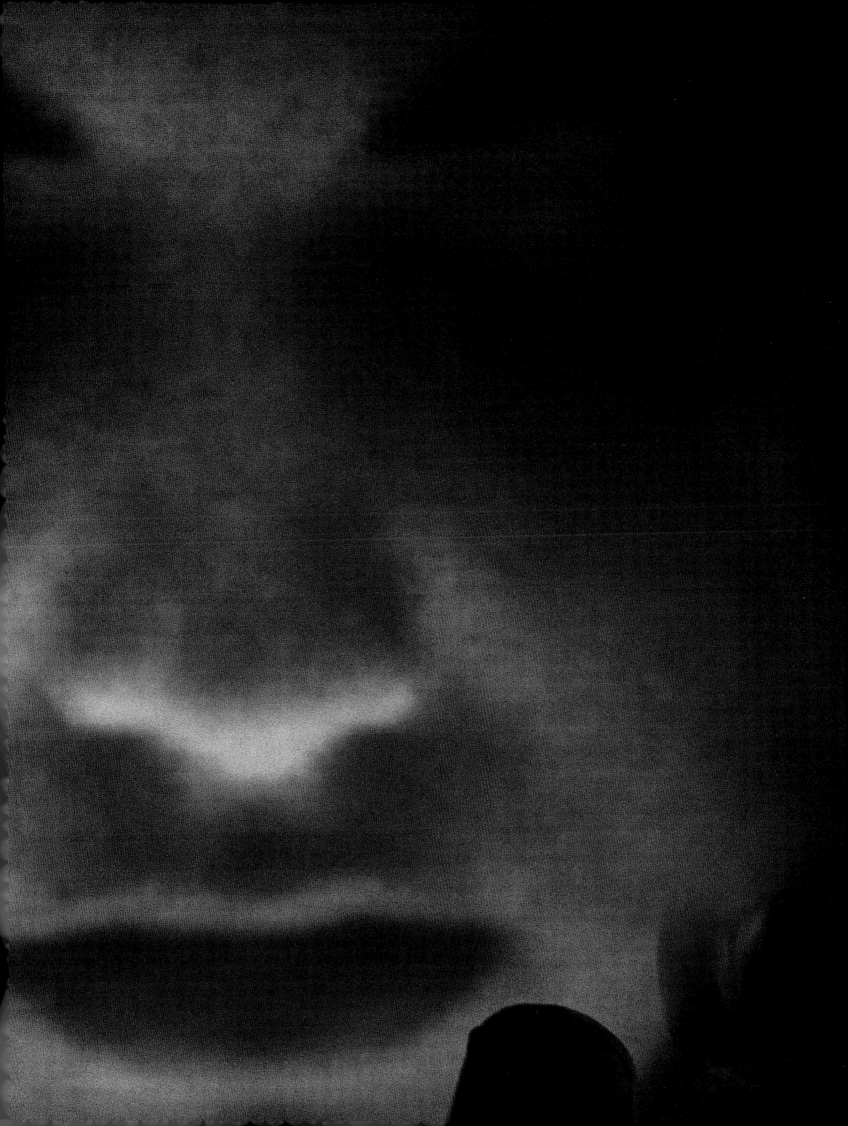

Places

MATVRA

JEHAN · FRELLON
L Y O N S

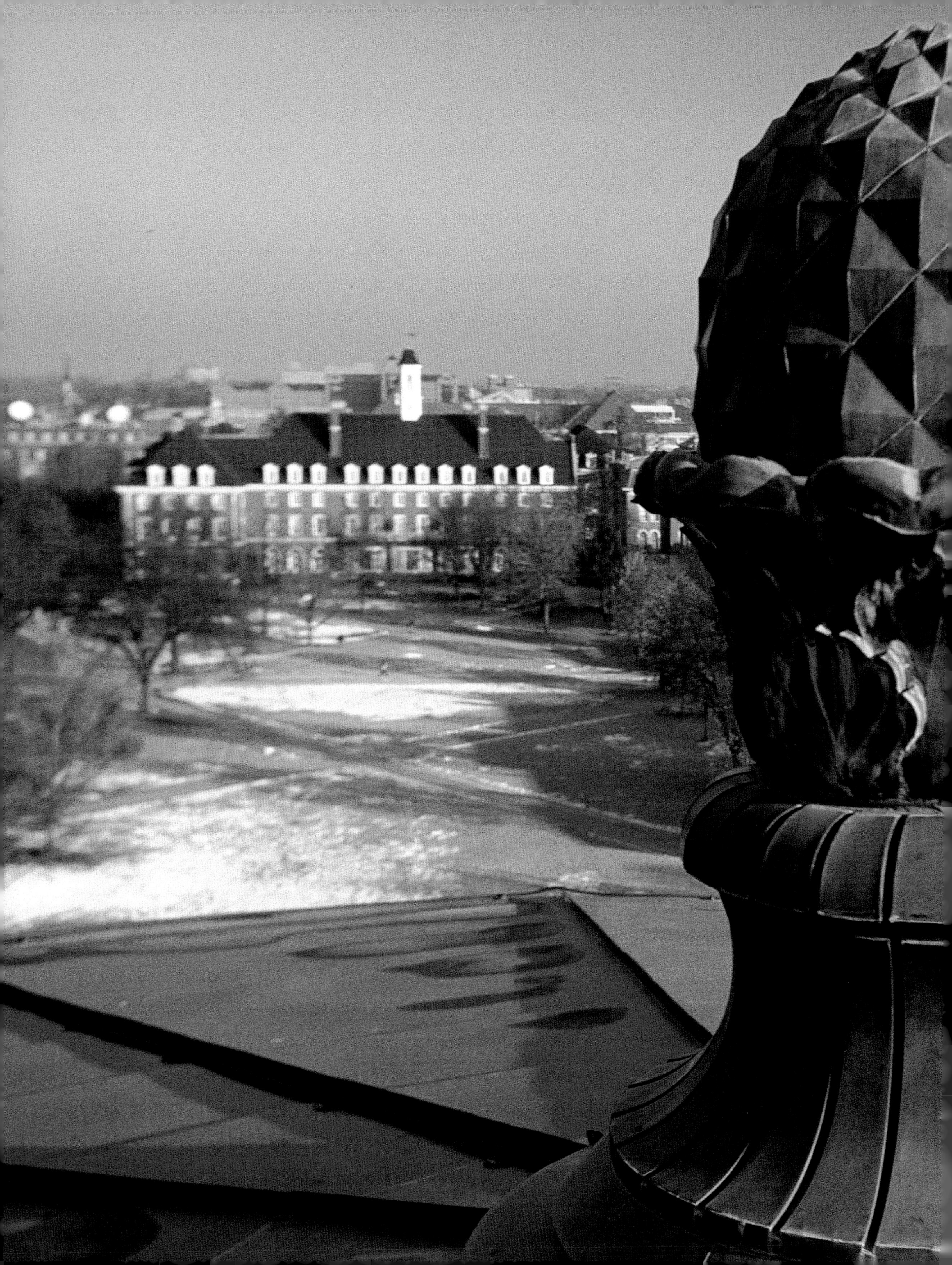

Colors

1867

Shortly after the Illinois Industrial University opened on March 2, 1868, a country-doctor's son named James Newton Matthews walked into the five-story seminary building that served as its campus. He probably didn't know that he was about to become the first enrolled student of that first class, "the Class of 1872," and he certainly didn't know that in less than two decades the institution (which had been chartered by the Legislature the year before he arrived) would be reborn as the University of Illinois. Since in those days cows and pigs wandered the muddy fields between Urbana and Champaign, chances are he felt, if not at home, then at least in comfortably familiar surroundings.

Matthews was 15 years old that late-winter day, and had been writing poetry since he was 11. He was one of 50 young men welcomed that year by the faculty, which consisted of two Eastern-educated professors and a supplementary "head farmer" from Chicago. A horse-drawn streetcar carried passengers between Champaign and Urbana, and the seminary building offered nourishing spaces for a life of the mind: recitation rooms, library, offices, chapel, dormitories, kitchen, and dining room. Soon after, the trustees approved $7,850 to fence off the site, add a portico, rearrange some rooms, and grade the grounds.

In the years following the Civil War, there was plenty of demand for higher education, and plenty of dissatisfaction with the church-based and classical colleges then providing it. ("As stagnant as a Spanish convent and as self-satisfied as a Bourbon duchy," grumbled one contemporary observer.) The Industrial Age, (and the clamor for practical education to support both industry and agriculture) was steaming ahead.

Yet the University's earliest leaders (including Jonathan Milton Gregory, its first president) made it clear that their mission lay beyond the purely practical task of educating engineers, industrialists, and farmers. They would teach the fundamental sciences, mathematics, Greek, Latin, modern languages and the social sciences. Also on the curriculum was religion (and its dour companion, mandatory chapel), military tactics (required by the federal Land Grant Act, which had enabled the Illinois legislature to authorize the University), and manual labor (still represented on the University's seal: Learning & Labor). But those requirements gradually disappeared from the curriculum as the cultural climate evolved.

Twenty young men graduated in that first Class of '72, by which time the University had already been open to women for two years. At the head of the class was Matthews, who had studied English language and literature; served as editor of The Student; and helped organize the Philomathean Literary Society. He worked as a journalist for two years before going off to the Medical College of St. Louis, graduating in 1878.

On returning to Effingham County to take over his late father's practice, Matthews treated his patients with skill and compassion for more than three decades. "He went forth as a physician and ministered like a priest," wrote a friend and fellow writer named William Hurt. "He healed the heart as well as the body." But like another doctor named William Carlos Williams, Matthews is remembered today not for his medical skills but for his way with words. He became known as the "Poet of the Prairie" and the "Singing Poet", "Thou meadowlark no less than nightingale," in the words of his friend and fellow poet James Whitcomb Riley, who hailed him as "Bard of our Western World." He was the "Western Warbler" to William Hurt, who wrote: "When Matthews sings the soul takes wings/And soars above all sordid things." Yet Matthews' joyful, down-to-earth touch is still evident in his poem "The Old Housefly," which celebrated the seasonal return of an insect most regard as a pest:

> "I love to see him tilting on his slender, tender toes, I love to watch him bump and buzz and balance on his nose."

He published several books of poetry during his lifetime, including Tempe Vale and Other Poems and The Lute of Life.

In 1910, a few days after walking five miles through foul weather to attend to a sick patient, Matthews died of a heart ailment aggravated by pneumonia. He was "one of the knightliest souls I ever knew," wrote Hurt, and a "man of almost shrinking modesty. In an age of self-assertion and auto-aggrandizement, he stood abashed at the approach of Fame." One likes to think that he would not have been abashed at the growing fame of the University of Illinois, whose remarkable adventure in higher education began with him.

Details

PRELUDE

Sunset and open sky transform the gracefully pleated roof of Assembly Hall from white to **Orange and Blue.**

Spring corn stretches to the horizon on the **South Farms**. The "outdoor laboratory" of more than 2,700 acres is owned by the College of Agricultural, Consumer and Environmental Sciences.

Nearly **26,000 pairs of undergraduate feet** walk (or recline) on the grounds of the Urbana campus each year.

A band member's cape reflected in the **horn of a sousaphone**, often confused with its close relative, the tuba. The first college band to use the sousaphone? None other than the Marching Illini.

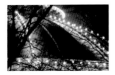

Afternoon in the foyer of the Krannert Center for the Performing Arts' acoustically superior **Foellinger Great Hall**. Made possible by the generous gift of Herman Krannert '12 and his wife, Ellnora, the Center is a stunning architectural achievement designed by University of Illinois alumnus and Lincoln Center designer Max Abramovitz.

The glowing copper dome of the Foellinger Auditorium lends a feeling of **warmth and romance** to a foggy December night.

MOMENTS

page 21   Peak autumn leaves on a perfect **October day**. The network of bike paths through campus totals over six miles, including this stretch behind Foellinger Auditorium.

page 22   With poise and power, **a kicker strides in** to split the uprights, earning another three points for the Illini.

page 24   "What is the hardest thing in the world? **To think.**" Ralph Waldo Emerson.

page 26   The **Union's South Lounge** has always been a great place to dig into one's studies, or to lose oneself in a dream.

page 27   From its humble beginnings in 1868 of 644 books and government pamphlets, the University Library has grown into **the third largest academic library** in the country, with more than 9.5 million volumes.

page 28   According to official records, no tornado has ever touched down on campus, yet a **funnel cloud appears** to have swept through this dorm room in Allen Hall.

page 29   Before facing a matinee audience at the Krannert Center for the Performing Arts, a young **actor tends to details**. With numerous rehearsal halls, studios, classrooms, and prop, scenery, and costume shops filling its three subterranean levels, the Center provides extraordinary support for productions of every kind.

page 30   Innovative collaborations and **artistic exploration** has long characterized the Dance Program. Dance has been offered as a major at the U of I since 1949.

pages 32 and 33   **Posing** and picture taking are as traditional as the mortarboard itself.

pages 34 and 35   The University annually enrolls approximately 26,000 undergraduate and 10,000 graduate and professional students; more than 9,000 complete **bachelor's, master's, doctoral** and professional degrees each year.

page 36   A solitary dancer does a **stretch on the barre** in arabesque.

page 37   Clockwise from left: **Nobel Laureate Jack Kilby,** '47, co-inventor of the integrated circuit, addresses an audience at the Beckman Institute; students gather prior to a **Homecoming Parade;** an operation in the surgical ward at the College of Veterinary Medicine's Teaching Hospital. The UI **College of Veterinary Medicine**, established in 1948, is one of only 27 in the United States; **enjoying the warmth** of the Union on a cold winter's day.

page 38   A student pilot from the UI Institute of Aviation logs some flight time **above the clouds**. More than 50 years old, the Institute has produced 10,000 graduates, including astronaut Steve Nagel.

page 39   Memorial Stadium's **17 miles of seating** can accomodate up to 70,000 fans.

page 40   Top: Somewhere in this photo is a loose head prop...a scrumhalf...a fly-half...a lock. Together, they make up the **women's rugby** team, whose smart and fearless play has taken them as high as #3 in the nation. Bottom: Since performing at the nation's very first half-time show, during a 1907 game against the University of Chicago in Champaign, the **Marching Illini** have been dazzling audiences with their precision and inventiveness.

page 41   The women's **basketball team huddles** during a break in the action. Women have participated in NCAA-sanctioned sports since 1981, fielding teams in basketball, gymnastics, and softball, among others.

page 42   The **baton twirler** is a critical component of any marching band. During the football season, the Marching Illini Band practices its routines six days a week.
page 43   Top: For more than 90 years, **the Block I pep** club has been an important presence at Fighting Illini football games. Bottom: Players wait on the sideline of Memorial Stadium's Zuppke Field. The field is named for **legendary coach Bob Zuppke,** who led the Fighting Illini to four national and seven Big Ten titles during his tenure, 1913-1941.

page 44   Wheelchair athletes **streak across the prairie** during a training session. UI has fielded numerous national and world championship teams in wheelchair sports, and its Department of Rehabilitation-Education Services helped develop the first set of architectural accessibility standards.

page 46   A spontaneous January football game becomes a **motion study** in the flat light of late afternoon.

page 48   Nothing clears **the cobwebs of sleep** better than a long walk to class on a crisp fall morning.

PLACES

page 51   Morning sunlight floods the University Quad as another fall day begins on campus. **The Quad** has been the heart of campus since the University was chartered in 1867.

page 52   Like the roots of this magnificent London Planetree, the University Library nurtures success in all the **various branches** of academic study at the U of I.

page 54   Altgeld Hall's carillon tower glimpsed through Alexander Liberman's, 15-ton steel **sculpture, "Mananaan,"** sited on the Bardeen Engineering Quadrangle.
page 55   The former **portal to University Hall**, built in 1873, now welcomes visitors to campus as the Hallene Gateway.

page 56   An autumn sunset burns the **tips of the trees** near the south entrance of the Illini Union, a campus gathering spot since its opening in 1941.

page 58   Clockwise from left: **Memorial Stadium** columns honor those from UI who died in World War I; Union south **cupola**; the **Law School** through blinds; reflection in a **Harker Hall window.**
page 59   The lobby of the Foellinger Auditorium provides a **safe haven** from which to view an early morning blizzard on the Quad.

page 60   The original works of the first University tower clock, built by mechanical engineering professor **Stillman Williams Robinson** and his students. Before it was presented by the Class of 1878 to what was then the Illinois Industrial University, missed appointments and overly long classes were the rule.

page 61   Students and faculty in the College of Commerce and Business Administration keep an eye on **the global economy** in Wohlers Hall, formerly known as Comm West.

page 62   Kinkead Pavilion, dedicated in October 1988, added 20,000 square feet to the **Krannert Art Museum.**

page 63   The first building on campus dedicated to a single college, Engineering Hall, at left, completed in 1894, was rededicated in the fall of 2000 after a two-year renovation that restored much of its **original grandeur.** (In background, Illini Union)

page 64   When the College of Law enrolled its first class of 39 students in 1897, neither of its two professors had a law degree. Housed in the Law Building since 1955, the college now has more than 600 students and a **stellar faculty**.

page 65   A classical Ionic column supports the entablature on Davenport Hall. Named for Eugene Davenport, Dean of Agriculture from 1895-1922, the original home of the Agriculture School bears this quote from former University President Andrew S. Draper: **"The wealth of Illinois is in her soil** and her strength lies in its intelligent development."

pages 66 and 67   Seen in **dramatic perspective,** facades of the Psychology Department Building, left, and the Computer and Systems Research Lab, right, seem to merge.

page 68   Clockwise from left: Southside of **Grainger**; view from the **ACES Library**; **Lincoln Hall**; Temple **Hoyne Buell** interior.

page 69   If you're exceptionally tall, you can enjoy a fine **skyline view** from this Library window.

page 70   The garden gate at the Japan House leads to a world that is much removed from the clatter and bustle of normal campus life. Here, students and others can learn about such things as the Japanese tea ceremony, **Zen aesthetics**, and ikebana or flower arranging.

page 72   Unfazed by the emotion of Lorado Taft's "Daughter of Pyrrha," a student hits the books outside the Main Library. **The sculpture is one of several** figures adorning the campus that were intended for Taft's "Fountain of Creation," unfinished at the time of his death in 1936.

page 73   Clockwise from left: **Lincoln Hall** lobby balustrade; the **printer's mark** of Jehan Frellon, of Lyons, along with those of 26 other early printers, adorn the windows in the reference room and over the grand staircases of the Main Library; view of **Union** from Foellinger; **Alma Mater** unfocused.

page 74   Home to architecture, landscape architecture and urban and regional planning, the ultra-modern **Temple Hoyne Buell** Hall is itself a teaching tool – the building's exposed structural inner-workings encourage closer examination. The sweeping central atrium promotes communal gathering – a fitting tribute to Mr. Buell, "the father" of the modern shopping center.

COLORS

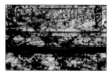

page 96   An Eastern Redbud blossoms on a **spring morning** in front of the Ceramics Building.

page 98   A planter outside the Animal Sciences Laboratory teems with marigolds–orange, of course. **Horticulturists plant** nearly 25,000 annuals each year in urns, planters and beds throughout the campus.

page 100   Everywhere around the University, the eye discovers **exquisite** architectural details. Kinkead Pavilion stairwell.
page 101   Clockwise from left: **Memorial Stadium**; Foellinger porch **balustrade**; Library **stairs**; Krannert Center **shadow**

page 102   Inside Assembly Hall, **fans rise to their feet** hoping for nothing but net. Completed in 1963, the Hall can hold up to 16,450 spectators.

page 104   This beautiful mosaic was uncovered and restored during renovations in Engineering Hall in 1999. It was **designed by Nathan Ricker**, creator of the Altgeld Hall door plates across the street.

page 106   Part of the pomp and circumstance of graduation day is the **commencement regalia.** The satin lining of the hood, worn by advanced degree recipients, designates the institution granting the degree.
page 107   Cheerleaders sprint down the field to **open the second half** of a football game at Memorial Stadium.

pages 108 and 109   With some **8,000 works of art** in its permanent collection, 13 galleries, and a variety of special exhibitions and events to mount, the curators at the Krannert Art Museum are constantly busy.

page 110   Alma Mater **Detail**
page 111   Students regularly take a shine to Lincoln, **rubbing his nose for luck** on their way to exams. The bronze bust by Hermon Atkins MacNeil has occupied its niche looking out the east entrance of Lincoln Hall since it was purchased in 1928.

page 112   Even in silhouette against the eerie glow of streetlights at 3 a.m., Altgeld Hall makes **a striking appearance**. The original building, completed in 1897, is a fine example of Richardsonian Romanesque architecture.

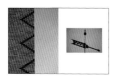

page 114   **Grainger** Library detail.
page 115   This bronze weather vane tops the Illini Union's open-arched north Cupola. The Union's designer, John Leavell, also designed the weather vane, which measures 8 feet tip to tip, and depicts the **phases of the moon** over three wigwams.

page 116 Evening falls outside the Illini Union's north portico.
page 117 Clockwise from left: **Old** technology; seeking **shelter**; **awaiting** students; bio-feedback **electrodes** in the Beckman Institute.

page 118 **Driving snow** obscures the Union in this view from Foellinger Auditorium.

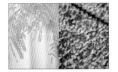

page 120 A **locust tree** displays its fall colors by Busey Hall. Completed in 1918 and originally known as the Women's Residence Hall, the building was renamed in 1937 to honor Mary E. Busey.
page 121 Annuals **bloom** in front of Foellinger Auditorium.

page 122 Postmodern columns on the Krannert Museum's **Kinkead Pavilion**.
page 123 The **15 bronze bells** in the bell tower of Altgeld Hall weigh a total of seven and one-half tons. They were cast by McShane Foundry, Baltimore, Maryland, and installed in the upper chamber of the bell tower in 1920.

page 124 Stately pines cast their shadows on the wall of the Krannert Center for the Performing Arts. University arborists tend **nearly 13,000 trees** on campus.

page 126 Alma Mater originally stood just south of Foellinger Auditorium, before moving to her present vantage point at the corner of Wright Street and Green Street in 1962. An inscription on the pedestal extends a warm welcome: "To the happy **children of the future** those of the past send greetings."

For

Fern, Nora and Wynne

and my Mother ('45) and Father

Thank you

Brian Stauffer '94 and Anna Flanagan for research and captions,
Sam Hughes (and Lex Tate '72) for "1867,"
and Roger Ebert '64 for generously contributing the Foreword.

Present and former UI Staff and Administration for help of all kinds:

Jason Lindsey and Debra Bolgla, and Chris Beuoy, Kent Brown, Jesse Evans,
Vanessa Faurie, Maureen Gilbert, Jim Gobberdiel, Amy Harten, Karen Hewitt,
Dave Johnson, Judy Jones, Kathleen Jones, Patricia Knowles, Don Kojich,
Anne Mansini, Lynette Marshall, Rebecca McBride, Jan McCracken, Carol Menaker,
Bill Murphy, Cyndi Paceley, Michele Plante, Jennifer Quirk, Joe Rank, David Riecks,
Ellen Swain, Richard Wilson, and Catherine Zech.

Photographers who worked as my assistants: Mario Morgado, Gary Grimaldi,
George W. Simmons, Bob Handelman, Edward Keating, Donald Vascimini,
Nicole Tausend, Philip Becker, and Brian Stauffer.

Friends Nadia and Fausto at Tank Design.